Audrey Ardern-Jones

Time in Pleats and Folds

Indigo Dreams Publishing

First Edition: Time in Pleats and Folds
First published in Great Britain in 2024 by:
Indigo Dreams Publishing
24, Forest Houses
Cookworthy Moor
Halwill
Beaworthy
Devon
EX21 5UU

www.indigodreamspublishing.com

Audrey Ardern-Jones has asserted her right under the
Copyright, Designs and Patents Act 1988 to be identified as the
author of this work.
© 2024 Audrey Ardern-Jones

ISBN 978-1-912876-87-7

British Library Cataloguing in Publication Data. A CIP record
for this book can be obtained from the British Library.

Designed and typeset in Palatino Linotype by Indigo Dreams.
Cover design by Ronnie Goodyer from an original painting by
@ Audrey Ardern-Jones.
Printed and bound in Great Britain by4edge Ltd.

Papers used by Indigo Dreams are recyclable products made
from wood grown in sustainable forests following the guidance
of the Forest Stewardship Council.

This book is dedicated to
Emily, Miri, Katie and Jamie.

*Much may be done in those little shreds
and patches of time which every day produces and which most
men throw away.*

~ Charles Caleb Colton

(1780-1832)

Also by Audrey Ardern-Jones

Doing the Rounds, IDP, 2019

CONTENTS

Time in Pleats and Folds

Time in Pleats and Folds

she touches the bark of trees on her way through the forest
the living is a passing traveller, the dead, a man come home
cones linger on the ground, each one a sculpture of its own
we are the same old dust of ten thousand ages
she knows the timelessness of the Gods hidden in these trees
the tree of immortality has crumbled to kindling wood
she picks up dropped needles to weave, counting minutes
when the green pines feel the coming of the spring
a shower of chaffinches burst into light, leaving us behind
looking back I sigh, looking before, I sigh again.

Lines in italics taken from "The Old Dust" by Li Bai, a 7th century Chinese poet.

Imaginings & Happenings
inspired by Thomas Lux

I've lived ghosts   all my life   spirits
      in quiet houses   quiet faces
images   of quietness   in packed cities
      in fog-pink smog
the rivers   the early mornings
      reflections in waters
clouds in skies   girls in petticoats
      a white buttered blur

I'm in a farm café   eating flapjacks
      I stare at brown velvet cattle
a disused wooden hut   where a bird
      flies out of an open door
the children feed apples   to a chestnut horse
      I notice a man   alone
at the next table   his face broken hearted
      I offer him a slice of cake

A Makeshift Diner

I want to show you this place,
it's tucked away in a nook of a long street,
it holds secrets of other landscapes, of other lives.

I want to show you this place,
so you see beyond the owner's deep-set eyes,
where you hear tunes of kindness in other languages.

I want to show you this place,
where there are hidden stories in the waitress's calm face
where memories of other lives live on in the titles of dishes.

I want to show you this place,
take you to a space where you'll raise your glass, celebrate
other worlds, a white rose on your table.

Take time out

bathe in warm seas every day
copper suns in rolling skies
notice tensions slip away

leave behind a world of grey
wake early and larks may rise
bathe in warm seas every day

dig up old stones in the way
hear the songbirds' lows and highs
notice tensions slip away

see the sun-ghosts leave and stay
gold-white shadows in disguise
bathe in warm seas every day

night-watch stars—see them stray
glints of light before the eyes
notice tensions slip away

it's fine to dream and to say
you're free—and your heart flies
bathe in warm seas every day
notice tensions slip away

In Silence

I'm fascinated by life: trees, clouds filling an empty sky,
the way a meadow-brown butterfly floats in silence.

I'm obsessed by lights: the night glow in a moon's eye,
the way sun's rays widen, mirages on water in silence.

I'm changed by songs: jazz, classical—low notes and high,
the way music transforms, pauses for moments in silence.

I'm riveted by rains: the African seasons of wet and dry,
the way land swims in water—land drenched in silence.

I'm captivated by seas: oceans, ships, high tides that mystify,
the way waves rush, push, shoals of fish swim in silence.

I'm enchanted by birds: swallows migrating with miles to fly,
the way birds arrive on my lawn, wait on branches in silence.

I'm energised by nature: the seasons of life—we're born to die,
the way each day surprises me, the joy of being in silence.

Tripped in the Rush, the Push

I disappear in my thoughts wondering	*pondering*
about the conversations I've missed	*wished*
by being always in a hurry persisting	*insisting*
in matters that probably don't matter	*flatter*
but for now I stare at snow falling	*slow dawning*
a stunning whiteness glosses bare trees	*fair breeze*
a brightness between gaps in dark skies	*sharp cries*
foxes & hedgehogs disappear in bushes	*shushes*
paw prints scatter &small birds huddle	*muddle*
in the crevices of stretched out branches	*dances*
and somehow this moment really matters	*shatters*

And this is now, now, the secret
"…to live moment by moment" ~ St Gianna Molla

I'm obsessed with superstitions:
I never say *happy birthday* early, never stick
chopsticks straight up, don't trim my nails
after the sun goes down and
carry an acorn in my pocket for luck.

The December light spills over me.
I see the ice-white glow on the apricot chest
of a robin, he's beside me in my garden,
I talk to him, a quizzical look in his eye—
I'm reinstated, alive.

January at the Fireside
inspired by Tchaikovsky's piano music from The Seasons

little steps   little steps   little steps
tiptoes of high notes   tiptoes of silences
come along   come along   come along
the winter's chill   the winter's frost
log fires filtering   streaking   crackling
see the light   feel the sparks   hear the spit
tiny birds on rooftops   tiny birds on wires
snowflakes swirling   dancing   somersaulting
little steps   little steps   tiptoes of high notes
tiptoes of silences   come along   come along

tiptoes of silences   come along   come along
little steps   little steps   tiptoes of high notes
snowflakes swirling   dancing   somersaulting
tiny birds on rooftops   tiny birds on wires
see the light   feel the sparks   hear the spit
log fires filtering   streaking   crackling
the winter's chill   the winter's frost
come along   come along   come along
tiptoes of high notes   tiptoes of silences
little steps   little steps   little steps

Because it's January

he hasn't shaved
he mends fences, digs trenches in the garden
wears shorts despite the cold—he knows
she's making marmalade
dicing orange peel into a copper pan
simmering juices in preparation
for another year

Ghazal—Voices

I'm a child on the edge of a precipice seeking lost voices,
voices of my Polish family never mentioned—hidden voices.

We think about the need to know—to live is to breathe,
to breathe is to be, to understand truths of our inner voices.

I'm unravelling my mother's story, why she chose to leave,
leave her other life, marry my father in a Mass of Latin voices.

I search names of my missing grandparents—names to receive,
receive: Marcel, Rosa, Laura—mother's siblings unheard voices.

I imagine Lvów's freeze in WWII, how white deceives,
deceives the innocent—bodies in snowflakes, silenced voices.

I feel the aura of angel-ghosts inside myself, know I believe,
believe in other worlds—the wind sings in whispered voices.

Wartime *Coup de Foudre*
for my parents

I think of Father, his wicked smile, dark wavy curls
and Mother with her powdered face, red lipstick
and deep gravel voice—they first met in a train,
she a translator and he a liason officer in the army.

I'd love to have seen the tempo of that first look,
eyes lingering, lashes flickering, lips shimmering,
how the world turned upside down, sideways,
how in that moment time lasted beyond a moment.

They say new love takes over, how love stuns in
ways of bees, the buzz of sting—how love flows
through other worlds, spins suns, speeds up madness,
dizzies one into a wild stupor of carelessness.

Months later they made vows in Jaffa on a warm
November day. He gave her an engraved platinum ring,
she gave him tears and her essence. And love lasted
a lifetime despite setbacks, gunshots echoing.

Firstborn

me her baby the doctors advised
to abort, she a refugee with TB
in her right kidney—she who wanted
me to be here more than herself,
who named me Audrey after my English
grandmother a lady with white hair
a heart of scented hyacinths, snowdrops,
she who cared for me during the long
months and weeks of separation after
my birth, the lengthy days of my mother's
hospitalisation, of isolation, recovery
a baby that seemed to all a miracle

She was the Image of Marlene

La vie en rose her favourite song
hair curled in clouds of smoke,
white gloves and a long, black holder,
like *Marlene* she spoke English
with a thick-honey accent.
I loved to light Mother's cigarette,
flick her gold lighter twice,
see her wince, breathe in.

She smoked all day despite TB,
breast cancer, warnings from doctors.
She wheezed into radiotherapy,
metastasis squeezing her lungs.
After forty-six years she quit smoking
became a TV addict of cricket and snooker.

A Miracle of Timings

My mother shares a video with two Polish priests,
they're watching Pope John Paul's visit to the UK,
memories of the first ever Polish Pope on tour.

They're drinking wine, eating plates of *pązki*,
babka drożdżowa and her favourite dish *szarlotka*,
they're celebrating endings and new beginnings.

Mother speaks in Polish for the first time in ages,
Father sheltered her from others fearing she might
crack up again—like she did after the war.

The front doorbell rings and the postman drops
a letter with Polish stamps—scrawled writing,
the address crossed out, redirected many times.

It's from Helena her sister, unheard of in years,
scrambled words in Polish about holy devotions
to the Black Madonna—a plea to get in touch.

Fr Stanislaw reads out each page as mother sobs,
Fr Antoni calls up Warsaw and Helena answers—
the sisters speak in stammers and stuttered tears,

each thinking back to the last time they were together,
Helena playing Chopin's Preludes on the piano,
the shutters shut, darkness on the horizon, closing in.

pączki –doughnuts; babka drożdżowa – yeast cakes
szarlotka – traditional Polish Apple pie

Mother Sick in Bed

I take her temperature under the arm
with an ancient glass thermometer—
I wash her flushed face with an ice-cold
flannel—plump up the pillows and hold
her upright, rub her back in anticlockwise
circles like I used to soothe my babies
after their feed. I change her nightdress
and remake the bed to cool her down—
We remind ourselves of our lives lived
in the sweltering heat—the time a snake
came in my bath. I thought this slimy,
wriggling creature was to be splashed
and played with—she yelled at me to jump
and run. I wasn't scared—I can still hear
the screams though she denies it as we speak.
I pour out lemon syrup, add in hot water
and a spoonful of Polish honey—I promise
her a tot of malt whisky when she's better.

A Trip through Lviv in 2017

Voices soak me, winds chip my face, my heart.
I'm on a tram trundling through the city, in my head
I hear Mother speaking in her broken English,

vill you sit by z vindow—maybe the lady opposite
is my relative, she has Mother's almond-shaped
azure-blue eyes, same nose and high cheekbones,

she's dressed in a belted black coat sitting next
to a young man who's the double of my brother,
tall with dark frizzy hair, a brown suede jacket.

I drift, think of lives lived here before the 1940's,
imagined family members—it's the look on their
faces reflected in a mirrored glass that stuns me.

I banish all thoughts and leave the tram, cross
over tracks to visit St Mary Magdalene's church.
As I enter, an aged nun smiles at me, collects money

in a brass dish. I listen to the choir singing songs,
contemplate this language of clustered consonants,
know soon I'll sip Żubrówka from a cracked glass.

My Mother's House Speaks

I was once part of Austria, Poland—now Ukraine,
my maker sculpted me into a beauty, walls with
with curls and curves, my tall windows grace
a cloudless blue sky—grilled black balconies gird
my middle, my parapet is decorated in different
shapes and sizes, circles, arches, minute pillars
—a chestnut tree sweeps leaves across my face.

Sounds of tinkling piano music and a bandora's
plucked strings echo throughout my rooms—
pleated drapes hang over my windows, aromas
of *borscht* fill my kitchen. I've lived days of lavish
culture, braved years of swastikas defacing walls.
Families have hidden in sewers in my rat-infested
basement—lives saved, reinstated and renamed.

Your mother loved this place—most mornings
she'd skip down my steps holding her father's
hand, strolling to the bakery—she used to brush
your grandmother's auburn hair in my main
upstairs bedroom, arrange it in a curled topknot.
These days I'm torn apart, stairs divide me up.
I'm an heirloom, a survivor in a troubled city.

They Offer Themselves Up
February 2022

Old people armed with guns and coffee cups,
teenagers in Liverpool's football T-shirts,
artists, musicians, bus drivers, anyone from
anywhere who'll brave it, drive the enemy out.

Today, forests fill with the putrid stench of war,
resistance soldiers fight for freedom, wear
helmets, cower in tanks—cities howl, bomb-blasted
buildings crumble, debris scattered far and wide.

This place hides my history of unmarked graves,
fields of bones buried deep underground, faces
I never knew. In my head I hear my mother
imploring the Russian soldiers to exit now.

Testament

after the poet Taras Shevchenko

I'd like to see the gold-domed monasteries
in Kyiv's city centre and bow my head
to the choirs of monks chanting
and praying for peace. I dream of being
in a starlit sky high over Taras Hill, where
I'll feel the beat of Shevchenko's heart
bury my thoughts in poetry, honey & hope

I'll soak myself in the Dnipro,
feel the freshness of water over my face,
lose myself in a beautiful river

I'm angry at the brutality of Putin's army,
the hurt of innocents, the exodus of lives
to other countries. Birds wait, brood in darkness.
Zelensky warns *when you attack us, you will see
our faces.* Like Taras, the people of Ukraine
never give up. Marigolds and sunflowers
in pouring rain gain strength, live on

bury my thoughts in poetry, honey & hope
lose myself in a beautiful river,
in pouring rain gain strength, live on

Child in Transit

I see her on the news—a small blonde girl
wearing a pink anorak, white bobble hat,
her nose pressed on the train's windowpane.

She's in a carriage bursting with mothers
holding babies and stuffed toys—she taps
on the glass and blows kisses to her father.

He's there in the crowd on the platform
waving and running as the train chugs away;
everywhere people are pushing and shouting.

This is Kharkiv where air has lost its breath,
where figures fade into the distance—disappear
and where birds have left their nests.

Today in March

For Daniel aged 9 who has lived in England for a year

I see daffodils everywhere, yellow flowers
in gardens, parks and in a vase in our kitchen.
Yellow like the sun, like the colour of sunflowers
the symbol of my homeland. Some days I long
to be back home walking in the countryside
with my grandpa and my two grannies and a dog
called Matviy. But for now I must go to school,
play with new friends and learn about England.
I speak English like an English boy, but my heart
is Ukrainian. I hope soon that this war will end,
and that we'll rebuild our burnt-out cities,
our burnt-out hearts and afterwards, everywhere
we'll see yellow flowers in our gardens, parks
and in a vase in our kitchen.

My Nightmare Tossed in a Haibun

It's night, the moon a Eucharistic host. I'm asleep and I dream I meet Sara my grandma— she has blank-gold eyes and they stare down at me: she's sitting on a branch of a tree, her red hair plaited over her head. Her voice is a chorus of violin chords and her face a Baba Yaga face of mischief and menace. Our ginger cat Jasper is there, looking up at the tree and is resting on a yellow-velvet cushion. My tall, handsome Polish/Ukrainian grandfather walks out through a window & greets me with a hug.

    inside each of us
    images voyage elsewhere
    upturn the dark thoughts

Sevenling
in memory of the poet Roddy Lumsden

He loved the pub—chatting
to young poets, ginger cake
and *Close Cover* by Wim Mertens.

He couldn't abide show-offs,
waking early in the morning,
pompous poets on social media.

He should have won the Eliot Prize.

Vespertina Quiesa

After a portrait of a young woman by Edward Coley Burne-Jones

You stand alone in a grass courtyard leaning
against a red fence. You remind me of my
seventeen year-old self, have my auburn hair.
You wear clothes that I love: a black lace
gown over a velvet emerald dress. You look
pensive. Are you thinking of becoming a nun?
The high stone buildings in the background
look like a convent. I imagine Mother Novitiate
waits for you somewhere in the cloisters.

The world tugs at you, like it did for me, tugs
at the ring you're holding on your little finger.
I once thought I might join a silent order, wake
early, sing psalms in the chapel, grow herbs
in the kitchen garden, have a patch of purple
foxgloves outside my bedroom window. My
brother said I'd talk too much, miss dancing
and wearing makeup. You must listen to your
heart, let chance decide, the way it always does.

Convent Girls Catching Up

We're in a city bar drinking piña coladas
and margaritas, we haven't seen each other
in years—we gossip about our school life,
recalling the day when Sister Scholastica
swooped into our classroom, bent black
wings flapping, face scowling as she told
us off for singing our hearts out to the
Beatles latest song *Ob-La-Di, Ob-La-Da.*

Linda's face is a map of lines, her voice
a yellow tang of lemons. Pippa's tune is quiet,
grey hair tied in a bun, tell-tale bags under
her eyes. Stella talks of therapy, marriages
and time in recovery. Jill streaks her hair pink,
chats about a creep she met on a singles app,
she gave him money for his mother's cancer
treatment in Barbados. His mother lives here.

We chat about the awfulness of scammers.
I tell them how I play the scumbags at their
own game speaking in funny accents and
talking gibberish. We celebrate our teenage
years of another age—Mary Quant and Dusty
Springfield's pink-white lipstick, thick-fringe
hair and tick-black eyes. We leave this place
humming Dusty's song *Once upon a time.*

Night Duty

I take a break—stare at midnight life
outside my hospital in Mortimer Street.
I see couples kissing, kids waving down cabs
at the lights—tramps settled in doorways,
rubbish bags are piled high on street corners.

The consultant's car park is almost empty,
I glimpse the head porter checking the spaces
for troublemakers. He's wearing a peaked cap,
has brass buttons on a green coat, he's out
there smoking under the glare of a full moon.

I gaze down at this other world away from
patients, bedpans, oxygen masks and bleeps
of machines—the catheter bags need to be
emptied into the plastic jugs left in the sluice.
It's my birthday tomorrow, I'm nineteen.

Girl in Bed

After the painting by Lucien Freud

You remind me of a sixteen-year-old girl with leukaemia
I nursed years ago—something about the shape of your face,
the lapis-blue colour and the size of your eyes, corners

of your rose-pink mouth. You're propped up by your elbow,
naked shoulders above a plush eiderdown, a pale halo
surrounds your head—I like the way your blonde hair flicks

neatly under a cupped hand, tiny indigo veins track a route
on an open wrist, undamaged unlike my patient's bandaged
chemo-infused arms—I think back to when I read her poetry

in her quiet room of isolation, as she, like you rested her head
on a large pillow, she believed in Roger's poem: *Bees cannot fly,*
the lines of *wing-span* and *body weight,* the miracle *but they do.*

I wonder what you're thinking as Lucian paints you, does
your mother know where you are? You look angelic, so perfect,
but I see loneliness in your long fingers and half-bitten nails.

Locked Inside

Fingers like claws of ice, a tiny sparrow of a lady in
a wheelchair waiting for me, the Twilight Nurse.

Her husband introduces his wife—he has pencil-thin
lips, pencil-thin moustache and a voice that booms.

She listens, her head angled on one side: no words,
a sound of nothingness—her bottom lip curling

round a corner, wet tears speak through dark brown
eyes. I take her upstairs on a chair-lift—bits of soap

sit on her pink basin. I change her catheter bag, talk
gently as I dress her ulcerated legs, wash her—notice

how she trembles when her husband's name is spoken,
notice her long uncut nails, scratches on both arms.

I speak about the faded photo on the dressing table,
a girl like Audrey Hepburn in a pale lemon dress

sitting in the midst of three girls—I ask if they are all
sisters, and she's the one in the middle—she nods.

I promise to be there for her: to help this tiny sparrow
fly outside the window—arrange for Judy to set her hair.

The Blood Room

I take blood in this room. Vincent's chair stares
down at us. Perhaps Ray from Works has hung it
too high. I adore this print, wish I was in Arles or
Saint-Remy-de-Provence with a bottle of rosé in
my kitchen. Maria shares this room with me. I'm
new, she doesn't approve of me or the machine
I've installed — harp music on tape to settle cancer
patients having bloods taken. She disapproves of
my chat. Instead, she likes to busy herself wiping
surfaces with spirit, counting syringes and bottles.
I've told her how the pipe in the painting reminds
me of my grandfather – how he suffered depression
after his child Oliver died aged eleven. He left us
before I was born. I'm calmed by the strawness of
the chair, the pink and green brushstrokes tinged
with gold that outline its shape — there's something
about the way the bulbs lean out in Vincent's box.
I'd like to pick up the pouch of tobacco, fill the pipe,
light it and smell the meadow-sweet scent, see my
grandfather puff smoke curls, like the man in my
photo. I love this chair, love that no-one sits on it.

Nancy Can't Make up her Mind

I tell her it doesn't matter which one she chooses,
the apricot-orange purse, or the black and yellow
clutch bag with a platinum chain shoulder strap.

Her favourite is a basket covered in sea shells
spelling out her name—the trick is to know
what to say when she repeats, again and again

help me, help me, I don't like my mother, I like my father.
She sits in a high-back dark red chair, raised feet,
most days her bed remains unmade, she tells me

she'd like a hundred hands to hold her, how an
angel came to her at midnight and kissed a cheek.
I show photographs on my phone, neighbours

in the garden, Nigel cooking veggie sausages on
a barbeque—she laughs, clipping and re-clipping
the large gold clasp on her red plastic handbag.

I promise I'll be back soon—*please, don't leave me,
don't leave me, I don't like my mother, I like my father.*
Her voice lingers on through the long corridors.

The Woman in the Hospital Basement

We're strangers in a reception area of the cardiology unit,
our partners taken elsewhere as day cases. Visitors
banned from visiting—so we wait, turn pages in our
books, fidget, no-one says anything for ages.

Next to me sits a lady with a stick—she's not reading,
but gazing at the glossy white walls. She's wearing
a fuchsia pink beret on her head that catches my eye.
I comment on the time we'll need to wait and the time

we arrived this morning. She says he's a devil for being
early, so she'd been up at 5am. He's 88 and she's sure
he's losing it—he covers up well and she's worried
at this moment he's telling a pack of fibs to the doctors.

I look at a face that must have been pretty and imagine
her somewhere else, at a party in a pale pink crêpe
summer dress with silver beads round her neck in the
centre of a crowd, a chilled martini in her hand.

She's talking on and on—he's so selfish, doesn't do
anything to help her. No, she can't bother her daughter,
she's unwell, has mental problems, her son lives in France.
He wants them to visit—no she can't bear the thought of it,

though she'd like him to go, to give her a break, but
he won't go without her. I think of him holding forth
with the others in the day-ward. Like my husband,
he's different with the doctors, young again and charming.

Unstable Angina & Meanings of God & Other Lives

Red, yellow, green wires strapped on pads, monitors with bells and hisses—a heart in trouble. My husband lies on a trolley amidst charts and monitors. A male nurse checks the screen, the rate now out of sync—I joke *at least he's not dead*. I think I'm in trouble. The nurse pulls the paper curtains round the bed, a whirlwind of cover hides us away. He stares me in the eyes, makes me want to laugh: in broken English he says: *you never die, you just transform, transform your being into another world* – it sounds easy, tantalising—he assures me, these views are not his, but *evidence based*. His face shoots arrows as he names scientific miracles on *YouTube*, papers he's seen recently published, out-of-body stories. I know that he shouldn't do this, he's out of order. I like his Spanish accent.

***

My husband's admitted where guys lie half-asleep in hospital beds. No-one speaks for hours. Suddenly, a young man with a spiky hairstyle and a breathless voice is curious. *Do you believe in God?* He asks the ward and looks at me, the female visitor. An old man with a grey ponytail and a posh Surrey accent answers: *I'm an atheist, there's no such thing as a God.* My husband chips in, shrugs his shoulders: *my grandfather was a lay preacher*—the chat travels on in strange places. The young man has yellow eyes, confesses he can't read says he's not sure about God. He buries his head under his sheets, later the porter collects him—plastic bags with his clothes balance on his knees, a hospital blanket covers him, he waves goodbye, says he's off to the hospice.

And Afterwards
for Paul

We stand in her hallway where a west wind finds
its way through the cracked porch: her Roberts radio
always on, now switched off in a new emptiness.

Aprons hang on pegs on the kitchen door, scraps
of recipes pinned on a wall, newspaper cuttings held
together by wooden clothes pegs, words circled in red.

We'll ditch company calendars sent every Christmas
by her husband's office: she was glad they remembered
him: thirty-four years since a clot stopped his heart.

We find wrapped gifts and the blue silk blouse bought
for her last birthday left in the drawer, waiting for best.
We don't dare bin her washed gold milk bottle-tops.

I save her beaded necklaces, bangles—the lemon
plastic one that popped when pulled and pushed.
I picture the children playing with them in our garden.

We stumble on a pencil entry in her diary written days
before she was whisked away in the ambulance. A note
scribbled across a double page—*Jimmy where are you?*

Mother-in-law's Last Laugh

After she died he meant to
sprinkle his mother's ashes
on the roses, as she loved
to come and stay and water
all his plants while telling
her grandchildren stories
about both wars, and how hard
it was when she was young.

Years later, he found her
in the garden shed, wrapped
in a plastic pot covered
with brown parcel paper
hidden amongst the croquet set,
old spades and wooden racquets.
He immediately summoned
all the family for a sprinkling party.

The funny thing is
the following year no roses
grew where her ashes
were scattered. Instead
the shed was covered
in blackberries and scented
honeysuckle—someone said
they could hear her laughing.

Father Died at 10am

on a Saturday morning, his heart just stopped
outside in the open air — the shock upset Mother
so much she couldn't talk, eat or cry.

She stayed at home curled up on a sofa, curtains
drawn — we made arrangements by telephone
before visiting Mr Hunt the funeral director.

He said he was unable to understand Mother's
request to lie on top of Father's coffin in the hearse
to the service in the church from our house.

In a curled Dorset accent Mr Hunt spoke in short,
sharp sentences informing Mother that in England
such ways are not safe and are not the custom.

She wouldn't agree — we decided to leave her be.
On the actual day, she came with us in the booked
limousine wearing a black silk dress, a mantilla.

In some ways I would have loved to have seen her
stretched out on top of Daddy's coffin — roses & lilies
spread over her — glorious and exotic, just like her.

Blues for Elizabeth

for Rumbles

She taught girls to write essays, poetry and how to act,
a feisty brunette who enjoyed dressing up, wearing a hat—
a popular English teacher who'd taken several degrees.

She thought she might die following her second op
and crossed her fingers before deciding on a burial plot—
she liked the idea of a place in the woods under the trees.

We said our goodbyes on the grass-covered ground,
holding bunches of pink rhododendrons—not a sound
but the song of a thrush in the hush of a breeze.

As they lowered the wicker casket we thought of a girl
who loved life, loved Louis's tune *What a wonderful world...*
a sun in an indigo sky, bluebells, the hum of wild bees.

April in Lockdown

Not a trace of white trails streaking this tranquil sky,
a pied wagtail on a rooftop stares at an empty street
where green-backed, yellow-breasted blue tits flit by
trilling like trebles in a choir, where wrens meet
wrens in scented shrubs and sparrows spin like dice
across the city, where thrushes sing from afar,
notes repeating in the hush, where raucous cries
of restless crows call out warnings: *arrh, arrh, arrh...*

In my garden a blackbird sings, his orange beak
opens wide like a chorister, he loves this calm—
a robin chirps in harmony, a trio of magpies shriek
hey, hey, hey... loud as an endless ringing alarm.
I'd love to be a bird in air, flying free for hours
winging my way to a meadow of wild flowers.

Counting Steps

It's the noise of the men digging and shouting
that I miss these days: the sight of yellow jackets
and red hats—they've been drumming the ground,
shaping the new walkway in our town centre.
Now we're cordoned off, kept out, as if by ropes
that surround our playground in the park. An eerie
silence fills this space. I'm on my allowed out
daily walk—I pass Dave's closed sweetshop where
cards fill its grimy windows—*babysitters needed,*
rooms for rent: there's a hush in the Magpie's garden,
and Peggy's Laundrette is empty. As I trundle
home I think about my life as a child in the village
of Mporokoso in Zambia—we had no vaccinations,
no sun lotion—the time I caught malaria, a child
of six—my parents never seemed to worry, never
seemed to flap.

I call you *My Girls*

the three of you sit on my bedroom window sill
above a yellow washbasin—you lean in my direction.

I speak to you most mornings: fanfares of white
and pink alongside a mass of deep magenta petals,

sprawling blooms threaded with gold veins,
stalks entwined in stalks, buds tucked under buds.

I chat to you about my Covid sagas, the unresponsive
internet, the broken washing machine, my lost filling.

My granddaughter Miri says I'm going barmy, assures
me orchids have no ears, no ways of knowing my voice.

I'm arguing my case—I find articles that confirm plants
do listen: *minute air bubbles fizzing, bursting.*

My Turn

I'm unprepared for the density
of sleep, of ache, nausea,
a salt-sweet metal taste in my mouth,
the cough, the temperature.

Like the whisper of a leaf
I'll live again—when the trees mumble
in the wind and I step outside,
morning dew on the grass.

Stranger in the Vaccination Queue

A lady in a fur coat with a German accent taps
me on my arm to tell me that my thick, curly
reddish hair reminds her of her *Mutti's* sister
Gerda, her auntie who lived with the family
in Leipzig during the second world war.

She tells me Gerda's tongue flipped beneath
a gap in the roof of her mouth, her hair twirled
in a plait on the side of her head. Every night
Gerda removed an iron leg brace, hid it under
the bed, rubbed grease over the blistered skin.

Gerda liked to sing as she tidied up the mess,
laugh as she played cards with everyone, whistle
as she made sausages & sauerkraut in the coal-lit
cold *Küche*. One day they came: *Hitler's orders:
no babies for cripples.* She vanished for weeks.

She came home, a wound deeper than the neat
black stitches sewn in the middle of her tummy.
She wouldn't speak for ages. We took it in turn
to hug her, sing to her, tell her she was the best
auntie, the best as any *Mutti* could be.

She had to decide

whether or not to plant the tulips
before the ground was frozen
the evenings were long

she pictured the sunny room
the sun-washed wall
the air held the hint of nippiness

a black dog lay on an old bed
it seemed to bring back all the shadows
and aches of a lifetime

she walked down a side stream
the bay was one long ripple
with hidden white starflowers

light emerging through the early fog
the smell of the cold
she did not want to leave it yet

Rondeau in a Phone Call
for Sue

it hurt speaking to you today
you mention cancer in your upbeat way—
inside me something slips to another place,
shadows in my heart, on my face
the sky dark grey

you make the storm ahead a drizzle—I say
there are ways to tone down the wind, play
with time: you're a sun in darkness,
          one of the loveliest of our human race,
it hurt speaking

there's thunder in the distance but you'll stay
doing what you always do—living the day,
making sponge cakes for the freezer, just in case;
you'll laugh, chat on the phone, fill every space
it hurt speaking

Fine del Giorno – End of the Day
for Gloria

She rinses tableware, empties pots,
sweeps the floor, wraps a shawl around
the shoulders of her father in a wheel-chair.

He threads a rosary through fragile fingers,
stares most of the day at Italian TV.
She's made *lasagne alla bolognese al forno*.

She feeds him spoon by spoon, he slurps
as he swallows, slurps as he drinks, knows
time's running out, knows at each meal

she'll tuck a napkin down the front of his top,
like the bib his grandson Lorenzo wears
when he guzzles his favourite *banana gelato*.

.

Unpicking Me

my granddaughters Emily & Katie/ wear my
old shirts/ paint with acrylics/ I've taught them
to use fingers/ upturn a canvas / let paint drip/

I love mishaps/ the time I left my hat on the train/
muddled my French/ *j'ai perdu ma tête*/ my head/
not my hat/ Monsieur seemed astonished/

at night I listen to Jacques Loussier's piano jazz/
think back to my Zambian childhood/ pale yellow
rhythms in darkness/ the tap-tapping of heavy rain/

I eat honey toast and strawberries at 6am/ wear
a straw hat in the sun/ freckles on my hands/ my nose/
red hair fading/ make my husband a cup of tea/

Neighbours Wrapped in a Sestina

We trundle down Chase Hill, bump into Vijay
in his shorts and T-shirt: we catch up with Kim
sitting on a wooden seat chatting to Mrs Marriott.
We walk towards the market and greet Harriet,
she's in a hurry: we pass the bakery where Tim
waves to us—at the flower stall we see Cllr Wray.

We call him Jim, he prefers Cllr James Wray,
a bald man with a pot belly unlike slim Vijay
who speed-walks the pavements. Artist Tim
is booked to paint a portrait of red-headed Kim
the next-door neighbour of Latin teacher Harriet,
she lives in the semi on the right of Mrs Marriott.

Doris talks about her dead husband Dr Marriott,
I'm not sure she liked him very much. James Wray
is part of a local running club along with Harriet;
on Sundays they have lunch at the Swan with Vijay
and his family—we and others, including Kim
walk in groups in the local woods except for Tim

whose wife Sylvie has had a recent stroke. Tim
pushes her in a wheelchair to visit Mrs Marriott,
where they will gossip and tell tales about Kim
and the ongoing saga concerning Councillor Wray,
his white parrot and divorce from Pam. Vijay
knows why she left in a rush—won't tell Harriet

nor anyone, he keeps secrets safe. Miss Harriet
searches books in the library for Sylvie and Tim,
they hope one day to travel again by train. Vijay
sometimes wears silk tops knowing Mrs Marriott
swoons when he does—he's invited by Cllr Wray
to a doo where Jim's gowned in red robes and Kim

dresses in a turquoise low-cut lace frock—Kim
boasts she's a singer in a band and asks Harriet
to introduce her to Ben, a nephew of Cllr Wray.
He's a jazz pianist—he plays at gigs where Tim
brings Sylvie and cakes are made by Mrs Marriott
and spinach samosas are dished up by Mrs Vijay.

Who are we all? Cllr Wray thinks we're friends, Kim
calls us *darlings*. Vijay says we're family—Harriett
believes in proximity: close like Tim and Mrs Marriott.

After Three Miscarriages & an Ectopic
for Debs & Jamie

We crossed our fingers, said novenas.
I found a five-leaf clover, kept it safe.
After the scan, we knew you were a boy,
a shrimp curled sideways in a womb.

Each month seemed sacred, bulging
kicks prodding a swollen tummy. We
sang to you, told you to hang on in,
held on to your knees, fists and feet.

After the Caesarean I saw you
wrapped tight in your mother's arms—
your piercing dark eyes gazing out,
a flush of black hair, soft as new grass.

You turned a dulled sky in the afternoon
into a kaleidoscope of multi-colours.
Nowadays, each time I see you, a whirl
fills my heart, lifts me like a balloon.

Paul's Memento
for Mike

On the desk he keeps paperclips inside an old brass
trinket box—it rests beside pencils, pens and rubbers.
The name Liverpool and an image of an ancient cross
is etched on the hinged, hill-shaped lid—Samuel,
Paul's great-grandfather passed down this gift to his
eldest son Joseph—Samuel is seen in a photograph
wearing a Panama hat and holding a walking stick
greeting King Edward at Lime Street Station—Joseph,
a lifelong teetotaller and a lay Methodist minister
bequeathed this box to his son Jimmy—Paul's Dad,
who in the War risked his life by kicking incendiary bombs
off the roof of his office block in Liverpool's docks.
I know Paul will polish this box again—make it shine
like a burning sun before he leaves it to Michael, knowing
one day, he too will pass it on—to one of his girls.
.

My Lineage

Inside my grandmother's house hangs a weathered family tree,
gold-leafed names and dates toned down in muted ink.
The wind loose, the wind was still, shaken out dead from tree and hill.

I search the Blue Mountains and Irish Hills for missing black
sheep and I find farmers in flint Shetland crofts hoarding wool.
I had walked on at the wind's will: I sat now, for the wind was still.

I cross streams and stone bridges in Wales extracting ancestors
steeped in male voice choirs, lay preachers hidden in valleys.
Between my knees my forehead was, my lips, drawn in said not Alas!

I admire my sixteenth-century uncles, one a metaphysical poet
living in Somerset, his brother Roland, an artist painting horses.
My naked ears heard the day pass, my hair was over in the grass.

I note my mother's name added in—Erna translated into Nan
so others never knew she was a foreigner, let alone a Catholic.
My eyes, wide open, had the run of some ten weeds to fix upon.

I count cousins—Fred, with his famous pubs in Australia.
Cynthia an anthropologist in Kenya, Clem a guru in California.
Among few, out of sun, the woodspurge flowered, three cups in one.

I update recent discoveries, names of my Polish grandparents,
my first cousin Zygmunt Butzinski—a notable communist spy.
From perfect grief there need not be wisdom or even memory.

I write in siblings: Oliver, Nicola and me—our trio; our three.
I add in tiny stars under each of my grandchildren's names.
One thing then learnt remains to me; the woodspurge has a cup of three.

Note: phrases in italics are by Dante Gabriel Rossetti from The Woodspurge.

When I die

take a strand of my hair
to Lviv and place it

in a bed of white scented lilacs
in this city of my ancestors

place my heart
in a landscape of skies

so that I may live on
in poetry and paintings

in the galaxies of stars
through the tempests of time

Acknowledgements

Many thanks to the publications where some of the poems, or versions of them, have first appeared: ARTEMISPoetry, Finished Creatures, Poetry Wivenhoe, The Hippocrates Book of the Brain, The Hippocrates Anthology, Reach Poetry, Southbank Poetry, Online Anthology in Lockdown (Plymouth University) Carol Ann Duffy's online Manchester University Lockdown Website, The Poetry School Website, Stanzas for Ukraine, Poetry School Form Laboratory. The Bell House Poetry Website.

Prize Winning and Commended Poems:
'Mother's Last Laugh' Poetry Space, 2013. 'The Woman in the Basement' Commended in Hippocrates Competition 2018. 'Unpicking me' in Dempsey & Windle Summer Competition 2019, Ghazal 'Winter's Voices' 3rd Prize Winner in the Roger McGough Poetry Prize in 2020. 'She Can't Make her Mind up' Ist Prize in Lord Whisky's Animal Sanctuary competition 2022. 'Rondeau in a Phone Call' (different version) commended by Dempsey & Windle, Summer 2023.

To the owner on the https://allpoetry.com/The-Old-Dust for the lines of the poet Li Bai. Thanks to Laila Anne Farnes for her form The Taylor for the poem 'Testament'. To Roger McGough for his poem 'Bees cannot Fly' referenced in my poem 'Girl in bed'. To 'The Intelligent Plant 2013 Journal' for quote in 'I call you my girls'. To author Elisabeth Strout and publishers Simons & Schuster 2011f for random lines taken from 'Olive Kitterage' for the poem 'She had to decide'. 'La vie en rose' written by Edith Piaf in 1947 in the poem 'She was the Image of Marlene.'

I am grateful to Coffee-House Poetry Anne-Marie Fyfe & Cahal Dallat for so many inspiring online writing courses where many of the poems in this book have been created and

commented on. Thanks to the Poetry School tutors for various
courses and to tutor Steve Komarnyckyj for his inspirational
translations of Ukrainian poems.

I'd like to thank all the wonderful poets, including Jean Hall,
Paul Stephenson, Sue Burge and Mimi Khalvati, for invaluable
advice and comments given during the process of this forever-
changing manuscript. Thanks to the Lambs for ongoing poetry
support. Thanks to Claire Dyer, Alex Josephy & Angela Kirby
for so kindly endorsing this book. Thanks as always to Lucas
Jordan (flute) and Fabricio Mattos (classical guitar) for their
continuing involvement with the Poetry & Music Ensemble.

For the generosity of those of you that invite me to read from
my book at various venues, in blogs or online – and
commission me to write poems for both local and international
projects, a very warm thank you.

Thanks more than I can say to my publishers Ronnie Goodyer
and Dawn Bauling for their patience and belief in me.

Finally, thanks to my husband Paul and my wonderful family
for their love and ongoing support for the many different
poetry projects I continue to enjoy and support.

*Profits from this book will be shared with The Royal Marsden Cancer
Charity & Survey Stands with Ukraine Charity.*

Indigo Dreams Publishing Ltd
24, Forest Houses
Cookworthy Moor
Halwill
Beaworthy
Devon
EX21 5UU
www.indigodreamspublishing.com